PRACTICAL
OCCULTISM

PRACTICAL OCCULTISM

and

Occultism versus the Occult Arts

By
H. P. BLAVATSKY

—— 1981 ——

THE THEOSOPHICAL
PUBLISHING HOUSE

Adyar, Madras, India

68, Great Russell St., London, WCIB 3BU, England

Wheaton, Illinois 60187, U.S.A.

First Edition 1948
Second Printing 1959
Third ,, 1967
Fourth ,, 1972
Fifth ,, 1975
Sixth ,, 1981

ISBN 0-8356-7124-0 (U.S.A.)

PRINTED IN INDIA

At the Vasanta Press, The Theosophical Society,
Adyar, Madras 600020

PRACTICAL OCCULTISM

IMPORTANT TO STUDENTS

THERE are many people who are looking for practical instruction in Occultism. It becomes necessary, therefore, to state once for all:

(*a*) The essential difference between theoretical and practical Occultism; or what is generally known as Theosophy on the one hand, and Occult science on the other, and:

(*b*) The nature of the difficulties involved in the study of the latter.

It is easy to become a Theosophist. Any person of average intellectual capacities, and a leaning toward the metaphysical; of pure, unselfish life, who finds more joy in

helping his neighbour than in receiving help
himself, one who is ever ready to sacrifice
his own pleasures for the sake of other
people; and who loves Truth, Goodness and
Wisdom for their own sake, not for the
benefit they may confer—is a Theosophist.

But it is quite another matter to put
oneself upon the path which leads to the
knowledge of what is good to do, as to
the right discrimination of good from evil;
a path which also leads a man to that power
through which he can do the good he
desires, often without even apparently lift-
ing a finger.

Moreover, there is one important fact
with which the student should be made
acquainted. Namely, the enormous, almost
limitless, responsibility assumed by the
teacher for the sake of the pupil. From

the Gurus of the East who teach openly
or secretly, down to the few Kabalists in
Western lands who undertake to teach the
rudiments of the Sacred Science to their
disciples—those Western Hierophants being
often themselves ignorant of the danger
they incur—one and all of those " Teachers "
are subject to the same inviolable law.
From the moment they begin *really* to
teach, from the instant they confer *any*
power—whether psychic, mental or physical
—on their pupils, they take upon themselves
all the sins of that pupil, in connection with
the Occult Sciences, whether of omission or
commission, until the moment when initiation makes the pupil a Master and responsible in his turn.   There is a weird and mystic
religious law, greatly reverenced and acted
upon in the Greek, half-forgotten in the

Roman Catholic, and absolutely extinct in
the Protestant Church. It dates from the
earliest days of Christianity and has its basis
in the law just stated, of which it was a
symbol and an expression. This is the
dogma of the absolute sacredness of the
relation between the god-parents who stand
sponsors for a child.[1] These tacitly take
upon themselves all the sins of the newly
baptized child—(anointed as at the initiation, a mystery truly!)—until the day when
the child becomes a responsible unit, knowing good and evil. Thus it is clear why
the " Teachers " are so reticent, and why
" Chelas " are required to serve a seven

[1] So holy is the connection thus formed deemed in
the Greek Church, that a marriage between god-parents
of the same child is regarded as the worst kind of incest,
is considered illegal and is dissolved by law; and this
absolute prohibition extends even to the children of one
of the sponsors as regards those of the other.

years' probation to prove their fitness, and develop the qualities necessary to the security of both Master and pupil.

Occultism is not magic. It is *comparatively* easy to learn the trick of spells and the methods of using the subtler, but still material, forces of physical nature; the powers of the animal soul in man are soon awakened; the forces which his love, his hate, his passion, can call into operation, are readily developed. But this is Black Magic—*Sorcery*. For it is the motive, *and the motive alone*, which makes any exercise of power become black, malignant, or white, beneficent Magic. It is impossible to employ *Spiritual* forces if there is the slightest tinge of selfishness remaining in the operator. For, unless the intention is entirely unalloyed, the spiritual will transform itself into the psychic, act on the astral plane, and dire results may be produced by it. The powers and forces of animal nature can equally be used by the selfish and revengeful, as by the unselfish and the all-forgiving; the powers and forces of spirit lend themselves only to the perfectly pure in heart—and this is DIVINE MAGIC.

What are then the conditions required to become a student of the "Divina Sapientia"? For let it be known that no such instruction can possibly be given unless these certain conditions are complied with, and rigorously carried out during the years of study. This is a *sine qua non*. No man can swim unless he enters deep water. No bird can fly unless its wings are grown, and it has space before it and courage to trust itself to the air. A man who will wield a two-edged sword, must be a thorough master of the blunt weapon, if he would not injure himself. or—what is worse—others, at the first attempt.

To give an approximate idea of the conditions under which alone the study of Divine Wisdom can be pursued with safety, that is, without danger that Divine will give place to Black Magic, a page is given from the "private rules", with which every instructor in the East is furnished. The few passages which follow are chosen from a great number and explained in brackets.·

1. The place selected for receiving instruction must be a spot calculated not to distract the mind, and filled with "influence-evolving" (magnetic) objects. The five sacred colours gathered in a circle must

be there among other things. The place
must be free from any malignant influences
hanging about in the air.

[The place must be set apart, and used for
no other purpose. The five " sacred colours "
are the prismatic hues arranged in a certain
way, as these colours are very magnetic. By
" malignant influences " are meant any distur-
bances through strifes, quarrels, bad feelings,
etc., as these are said to impress themselves
immediately on the astral light, *i.e.*, in the
atmosphere of the place, and to hang " about in
the air ". This first condition seems easy enough
to accomplish, yet—on further consideration,
it is one of the most difficult ones to obtain.]

2.   Before the disciple shall be permitted
to study " face to face ", he has to acquire
preliminary understanding in a select company of other lay *upasaka* (disciples), the
number of whom must be odd.

[" Face to face ", means in this instance a
study independent or apart from others, when

the disciple gets his instruction *face to face* either with himself (his higher, Divine Self) or—his guru. It is then only that each receives *his due* of information, according to the use he has made of his knowledge. This can happen only toward the end of the cycle of instruction.]

3. Before thou (the teacher) shalt impart to thy *Lanoo* (disciple) the good (holy) words of LAMRIN, or shall permit him " to make ready " for *Dubjed* thou shalt take care that his mind is thoroughly purified and at peace with all, especially *with his other Selves*. Otherwise the words of Wisdom and of the good Law shall scatter and be picked up by the winds.

[" Lamrin " is a work of practical instructions, by Tson-kha-pa, in two portions, one for ecclesiastical and exoteric purposes, the other for esoteric use. " To make ready " for *Dubjed*, is to prepare the vessels used for seership, such as mirrors and crystals. The " other selves " refers to the fellow-students. Unless the greatest harmony reigns among the learners, *no* success is possible. It is the teacher who makes the selections according to the magnetic and electric natures of the 'students, bringing together and adjusting most carefully the positive and the negative elements.]

4. The *upasaka* while studying must take care to be united as the fingers on one hand. Thou shalt impress upon their minds that whatever hurts one should hurt the others; and if the rejoicing of one finds no echo in the breasts of the others, then the required conditions are absent, and it is useless to proceed.

[This can hardly happen if the preliminary choice made was consistent with the magnetic requirements. It is known that chelas otherwise promising and fit for the reception of truth, had to wait for years on account of their temper and the impossibility they felt to put themselves *in tune* with their companions. For—]

5. The co-disciples must be tuned by the guru as the strings of a lute (*vina*), each different from the others, yet each emitting sounds in harmony with all. Collectively they must form a keyboard answering in all its parts to thy lightest touch (the touch of the Master). Thus their minds shall open for the harmonies of Wisdom, to vibrate as knowledge through each and all, resulting in effects pleasing to the presiding gods (tutelary or patron-angels) and useful to the Lanoo. So shall Wisdom be impressed for ever on their hearts and the harmony of the law shall never be broken.

6. Those who desire to acquire the knowledge leading to the *Siddhis* (occult powers) have to renounce all the vanities of life and of the world (here follows enumeration of the Siddhis).

7.   None can feel the difference between himself and his fellow-students, such as "I am the wisest", "I am more holy and pleasing to the teacher, or in my community, than my brother", etc.,—and remain an upasaka. His thoughts must be predominantly fixed upon his heart, chasing therefrom every hostile thought to any living being. It (the heart) must be full of the feeling of its non-separateness from the rest of beings as from all in Nature; otherwise no success can follow.

8.   A *Lanoo* (disciple) has to dread external living influence alone (magnetic emanations from living creatures). For this reason, while at one with all, in his *inner nature*, he must take care to separate his outer (external) body from every foreign influence: none must drink out of, or eat

in his cup but himself. He must avoid bodily contact (*i.e.*, being touched or touch) with human, as with animal being.

[No pet animals are permitted, and it is forbidden even to touch certain trees and plants. A disciple has to live, so to say, in his own atmosphere in order to individualise it for occult purposes.]

9. The mind must remain blunt to all but the universal truths in nature, lest the " Doctrine of the Heart " should become only the " Doctrine of the Eye " (*i.e.*, empty exoteric ritualism).

10. No animal food of whatever kind, nothing that has life in it, should be taken by the disciple. No wine, no spirits or opium should be used; for these are like the *Lhamaym* (evil spirits), who fasten upon the unwary, they devour the understanding.

2

[Wine and Spirits are supposed to contain and preserve the bad magnetism of all the men who helped in their fabrication; the meat of each animal, to preserve the psychic characteristics of its kind.]

11.   Meditation, abstinence, the observation of moral duties, gentle thoughts, good deeds and kind words, as goodwill to all and entire oblivion of Self, are the most efficacious means of obtaining knowledge and preparing for the reception of higher wisdom.

12.   It is only by virtue of a strict observance of the foregoing rules that a Lanoo can hope to acquire in good time the Siddhis of the Arhats, the growth which makes him become gradually One with the UNIVERSAL ALL.

These 12 extracts are taken from among some 73 rules, to enumerate which would

be useless as they would be meaningless in
Europe. But even these few are enough to
show the immensity of the difficulties which
beset the path of the would-be " Upasaka",
who has been born and bred in Western
lands.[1]

All Western, and especially English, edu-
cation is instinct with the principle of emu-
lation and strife; each boy is urged to learn
more quickly, to outstrip his companions,
and to surpass them in every possible way.
What is mis-called " friendly rivalry " is
assiduously cultivated, and the same spirit
is fostered and strengthened in every detail
of life.

---

[1] Be it remembered that *all* " Chelas ", even lay disciples, are called Upasaka until after their first initiation,
when they become Lanoo-Upasaka. To that day, even
those who belong to Lamaseries and are *set apart*, are
considered as " laymen "

With such ideas "educated into" him from his childhood, how can a Western bring himself to feel towards his co-students "as the fingers on one hand"? Those co-students, too, are not of his *own selection*, or chosen by himself from personal sympathy and appreciation. They are chosen by his teacher on far other grounds, and he who would be a student must *first* be strong enough to kill out in his heart all feelings of dislike and antipathy to others. How many Westerns are ready even to attempt this in earnest?

And then the details of daily life, the command not to touch even the hand of one's nearest and dearest. How contrary to Western notions of affection and good feeling! How cold and hard it seems. Egotistical too, people would say, to abstain from giving pleasure to others for the sake of one's own development. Well, let those who think so defer till another lifetime the attempt to enter the path in real earnest. But let them not glory in their own fancied unselfishness. For, in reality, it is only the seeming appearances which they allow to deceive them, the conventional notions, based on emotionalism and gush, or so-called courtesy, things of the unreal life, not the dictates of Truth.

But even putting aside these difficulties, which may be considered " external", though their importance is none the less great, how are students in the West to " attune themselves " to harmony as here required of them? So strong has personality grown in Europe and America, that there is no school of artists even whose members do not hate and are not jealous of each other. " Professional " hatred and envy have become proverbial; men seek each to benefit himself at all costs, and even the so-called courtesies of life are but a hollow mask covering these demons of hatred and jealousy.

In the East the spirit of " non-separateness " is inculcated as steadily from childhood up, as in the West the spirit of rivalry. Personal ambition, personal feelings and desires, are not encouraged to grow so rampant there. When the soil is naturally good, it is cultivated in the right way, and the child grows into a man in whom the habit of subordination of one's lower to one's higher Self is strong and powerful. In the West men think that their own likes and dislikes of other men and things are guiding principles for them to act upon even when they do not make of them the law of their lives and seek to impose them upon others.

Let those who complain that they have learned little in the Theosophical Society lay to heart the words written in an article in the *Path* for last February:—" The key in each degree is the *aspirant himself*." It is not " the fear of God " which is " the beginning of Wisdom," but the knowledge of SELF which is WISDOM ITSELF.

How grand and true appears, thus, to the student of Occultism who has commenced to realise some of the foregoing truths, the answer given by the Delphic Oracle to all who came seeking after Occult Wisdom— words repeated and enforced again and again by the wise Socrates:—MAN KNOW THYSELF. . . .

OCCULTISM
VERSUS
THE OCCULT ARTS

> "I oft have heard, but ne'er believed till now,
>   There are, who can by potent magic spells
>   Bend to their crooked purpose Nature's laws."
>
> —MILTON.

IN this month's "Correspondence" several letters testify to the strong impression produced on some minds by our last month's article, *Practical Occultism.* Such letters go far to prove and strengthen two logical conclusions.

(*a*) There are more well-educated and thoughtful men who believe in the existence of Occultism and Magic (the two differing vastly) than the modern materialist dreams of; and—

(*b*) That most of the believers (comprising many Theosophists) have no definite idea of the nature of Occultism, and confuse it with the Occult sciences in general, the " black art " included.

Their representations of the powers it confers upon man, and of the means to be used to acquire them, are as varied as they are fanciful. Some imagine that a master in the art, to show the way, is all that is needed to become a Zanoni. Others, that one has but to cross the Canal of Suez and go to India to bloom forth as a Roger Bacon or even a Count St. Germain. Many take for their ideal, Margrave with his ever-renewing youth, and care little for the soul as the price paid for it. Not a few, mistaking " Witch-of-Endorism ", pure and simple, for Occultism—" through the yawning Earth from Stygian gloom, call up the meagre ghosts to walks of light ", and want, on the strength of this feat, to be regarded as full-blown Adepts. "Ceremonial Magic", according to the rules mockingly laid down by Eliphas Levi, is another imagined *alter ego* of the philosophy of the Arhats of old. In short, the prisms through which Occultism appears, to those innocent of the philosophy, are as multicoloured and varied as human fancy can make them.

Will these candidates to Wisdom and Power feel very indignant if told the plain truth? It is not only useful, but it has now become *necessary* to disabuse most of them, and before it is too late. This truth may be said in a few words: There are not in the West half-a-dozen among the fervent hundreds who call themselves "Occultists" who have even an approximately correct idea of the nature of the science they

seek to master.   With a few exceptions, they
are all on the highway to Sorcery. Let
them restore some order in the chaos that
reigns in their minds before they protest
against this statement. Let them first learn
the true relation in which the Occult
Sciences stand to Occultism, and the difference between the two, and then feel wrath-
ful if they still think themselves right.
Meanwhile, let them learn that Occultism
differs from Magic and other secret Sciences
as the glorious sun does from a rush-light,
as the immutable and immortal Spirit of
Man—the reflection of the absolute, cause-
less and unknowable ALL—differs from the
mortal clay—the human body.

In our highly civilised West, where
modern languages have been formed, and
words coined, in the wake of ideas and

thoughts—as happened with every tongue—
the more the latter became materialised in
the cold atmosphere of Western selfishness
and its incessant chase after the goods of
this world, the less was there any need felt
for the production of new terms to express
that which was tacitly regarded as absolute
and exploded " superstition ".   Such words
could answer only to ideas which a cultured
man was scarcely supposed to harbour in
his mind.

" Magic ", a synonym for jugglery; " Sorcery ", an equivalent for crass ignorance;
and " Occultism ", the sorry relic of crack-
brained, mediæval Fire-philosophers, of the
Jacob Boehmes and the St. Martins, are
expressions believed more than amply suffi-
cient to cover the whole field of " thimble-
rigging ".   They are terms of contempt, and

used generally only in reference to the dross
and residues of the dark ages and its preced-
ing æons of paganism. Therefore have we
no terms in the English tongue to define
and shade the difference between such
abnormal powers, or the sciences that lead
to the acquisitions of them, with the nicety
possible in the Eastern languages—pre-
eminently the Sanskrit. What do the words
" miracle " and " enchantment " [words
identical in meaning after all, as both express the idea of producing wonderful things
by *breaking the laws of nature* (!!) as explained
by the accepted authorities] convey to the
minds of those who hear, or who pronounce
them? A Christian—" breaking of the laws
of nature " notwithstanding—while believ-
ing firmly in the *miracles*, because said to
have been produced by God through Moses

will either scout the enchantments performed by Pharaoh's magicians, or attribute
them to the devil. It is the latter whom
our pious enemies connect with Occultism,
while their impious foes, the infidels, laugh
at Moses, Magicians, and Occultists, and
would blush to give one serious thought to
such " superstitions ". This, because there
is no term in existence to show the difference; no words to express the lights and
shadows, and draw the line of demarcation
between the sublime and the true, the
absurd and the ridiculous. The latter are
the theological interpretations which teach
the " breaking of the laws of Nature " by
man, God, or devil; the former—the *scien-
tific* "miracles" and enchantments of Moses
and the Magicians *in accordance with natural
laws,* both having been learned in all the

3

Wisdom of the Sanctuaries, which were the
"Royal Societies" of those days—and in
true OCCULTISM. This last word is cer-
tainly misleading, translated as it stands
from the compound word *Gupta-Vidya*,
"Secret Knowledge". But the knowledge
of what? Some of the Sanskrit terms may
help us.

There are four (out of the many other)
names of the various kinds of Esoteric
Knowledge or Sciences given, even in the
exoteric Purānas. There is (1) *Yajna-Vidya*,[1]

[1] "The *Yajna*", say the Brahmans, "exists from eter-
nity, for it proceeded forth from the Supreme One. . .
in whom it lay dormant from ' *no* beginning '. It is the
key to the TRAIVIDYA, the thrice sacred science contain-
ed in the Rig verses, which teaches the Yagas or
sacrificial mysteries. ' The Yajna ' exists as an invisible
thing at all times; it is like the latent power of electri-
city in an electrifying machine, requiring only the operation of a suitable apparatus in order to be elicited. It is
supposed to extend from the *Ahavaniya* or sacrificial
fire to the heavens, forming a bridge or ladder by means

knowledge of the occult powers awakened
in nature by the performance of certain religious ceremonies and rites. (2) *Mahavidya*,
the "great knowledge", the magic of the
Kabalists and of the *Tantrika* worship, often
Sorcery of the worst description. (3) *Guhya-
Vidya*, knowledge of the mystic powers residing in Sound (Ether), hence in the Mantras
(chanted prayers or incantations), and
depending on the rhythm and melody used;
in other words, a magical performance
based on knowledge of the Forces of
Nature and their correlation; and (4)
ATMA-VIDYA, a term which is translated

of which the sacrificer can communicate with the world
of gods and spirits, and even ascend when alive to their
abodes."—Martin Haug's *Aitareya Brahmana*.

"This *Yajna* is again one of the forms of the Ākāsa;
and the mystic word calling it into existence and pro-
nounced mentally by the initiated Priest is the *Lost word*
receiving impulse through WILL POWER."—"Isis Unveil-
ed," vol. i, Intr. See *Aitareya Brahmana*, Haug.

simply " Knowledge of the Soul ", *true Wisdom* by the Orientalists, but which means far more.

This last is the only kind of Occultism that any Theosophist who admires " Light on the Path ", and who would be wise and unselfish, ought to strive after. All the rest is some branch of the " Occult Sciences ", *i.e.,* arts based on the knowledge of the ultimate essence of all things in the Kingdoms of Nature—such as minerals, plants and animals—hence of things pertaining to the realm of *material* nature, however invisible that essence may be, and howsoever much it has hitherto eluded the grasp of Science. Alchemy, Astrology, Occult Physiology, Chiromancy, exist in Nature, and the *exact* Sciences—perhaps so called, because they are found in this age of paradoxical

philosophies the reverse—have already dis-
covered not a few of the above *arts*. But
clairvoyance, symbolised in India as the
" Eye of Siva ", called in Japan " Infinite
Vision ", is *not* Hypnotism, the illegitimate
son of Mesmerism, and is not to be acquired
by such arts. All the others may be
mastered and results obtained, whether
good, bad, or indifferent; but *Atma-Vidya*
sets small value on them. It includes them
all and may even use them occasionally,
but it does so after purifying them of their
dross, for beneficent purposes, and taking
care to deprive them of every element of
selfish motive. Let us explain: Any man
or woman can set himself or herself to study
one or all of the above specified " Occult
Arts " without any great previous preparation, and even without adopting any too

restraining mode of life. One could even dispense with any lofty standard of morality. In the last case, of course, ten to one the student would blossom into a very decent kind of sorcerer, and tumble down headlong into black magic. But what can this matter? The *Voodoos* and the *Dugpas* eat, drink and are merry . over hecatombs of victims of their infernal arts. And so do the amiable gentlemen vivisectionists and the *diploma-ed* " Hypnotisers " of the Faculties of Medicine; the only difference between the two classes being that the Voodoos and Dugpas are *conscious*, and the Charcot-Richet crew *unconscious*, Sorcerers. Thus, since both have to reap the fruits of their labours and achievements in the black art, the Western practitioners should not have the punishment and reputation without the profits and enjoyments they may get therefrom. For we say it again, *hypnotism* and *vivisection* as practised in such Schools, are *Sorcery* pure and simple, *minus* a knowledge that the Voodoos and Dugpas enjoy, and which no Charcot-Richet can procure for himself in fifty years of hard study and experimental observation. Let, then, those who will dabble in magic, whether they understand its nature or not, but who find the rules imposed upon students too hard, and who, therefore, lay Atma-Vidya or Occultism aside—go without it. Let them become magicians by all means, even though they do become *Voodoos* and *Dugpas* for the next ten incarnations.

But the interest of our readers will probably centre on those who are invincibly attracted towards the "Occult", yet who neither realise the true nature of what they aspire towards, nor have they become passion-proof, far less, truly unselfish.

How about these unfortunates, we shall be asked, who are thus rent in twain by conflicting forces? For it has been said too often to need repetition, and the fact itself is patent to any observer, that when once the desire for Occultism has really awakened in a man's heart, there remains for him no hope of peace, no place of rest and comfort in all the world. He is driven out into the wild and desolate spaces of life by an ever-gnawing unrest he cannot quell. His heart is too full of passion and selfish desire to permit him to pass the Golden Gate; he cannot find rest or peace in ordinary life. Must he then inevitably fall into sorcery and black magic, and through many incarnations heap up for himself a terrible Karma? Is there no other road for him?

Indeed there is, we answer. Let him aspire to no higher than he feels able to accomplish. Let him not take a burden upon himself too heavy for him to carry. Without ever becoming a " Mahatma ", a Buddha or a Great Saint, let him study the philosophy and the " Science of Soul ", and he can become one of the modest benefactors of humanity, without any " superhuman " powers. *Siddhis* (or the Arhat powers) are only for those who are able to lead the life, to comply with the terrible sacrifices required for such a training, and to comply with them *to the very letter*. Let them know at once and remember always, that *true Occultism or Theosophy* is the " Great Renunciation of SELF ", unconditionally and absolutely, in thought as in action. It is ALTRUISM, and it throws him who practises it out of calculation of the ranks of the living altogether. "Not for himself, but for the world, he lives", as soon as he has pledged himself to the work. Much is forgiven during the first years of probation. But no sooner is he "accepted" than his personality must disappear, and he has to become *a mere beneficent force in Nature*. There are two poles for him after that, two paths, and no midward place of rest. He has either to ascend laboriously, step by step, often through numerous incarnations and *no Devachanic break*, the golden ladder leading to Mahatmaship (the *Arhat* or *Bodhisattva* condition),—or—he will let himself slide down the ladder at the first false step, and roll down into *Dugpaship*. . . .

All this is either unknown or left out of sight altogether. Indeed, one who is able to follow the silent evolution of the preliminary aspirations of the candidates often finds strange ideas quietly taking possession of their minds. There are those whose reasoning powers have been so distorted by foreign influences that they imagine that animal passions can be so sublimated and elevated that their fury, force, and fire can, so to speak, be turned inwards; that they can be stored and shut up in one's breast, until their energy is, not expanded, but turned toward higher and more holy purposes: namely, *until their collective and unexpanded strength enables their possessor to enter the true Sanctuary of the Soul* and stand therein in the presence of the *Master*—the HIGHER SELF. For this purpose they will not struggle with their passions nor slay them. They will simply, by a strong effort of will, put down the fierce flames and keep them at bay within their natures, allowing the fire to smoulder under a thin layer of ashes. They submit joyfully to the torture of the Spartan boy who allowed the fox to devour his entrails rather than part with it. Oh, poor blind visionaries!

As well hope that a band of drunken chimney-sweeps, hot and greasy from their work, may be shut up in a Sanctuary hung with pure white linen, and that instead of soiling and turning it by their presence into a heap of dirty shreds, they will become masters in and of the sacred recess, and finally emerge from it as immaculate as that recess. Why not imagine that a dozen of skunks imprisoned in the pure atmosphere

of a *Dgon-pa* (a monastery) can issue out
of it impregnated with all the perfumes
of the incenses used? . . . Strange aber-
ration of the human mind. Can it be so?
Let us argue.

The "Master" in the Sanctuary of our
souls is "the Higher Self"—the divine
spirit whose consciousness is based upon
and derived solely (at any rate during the
mortal life of the man in whom it is captive)
from the Mind, which we have agreed to
call the *Human Soul* (the "Spiritual Soul"
being the vehicle of Spirit). In its turn
the former (the *personal* or human soul) is a
compound, in its highest form, of spiritual
aspirations, volitions, and divine love; and
in its lower aspect, of animal desires and
terrestrial passions imparted to it by its
associations with its vehicle, the seat of all

these. It thus stands as a link and a medium between the animal nature of man which its higher reason seeks to subdue, and his divine spiritual nature to which it gravitates, whenever it has the upper hand in its struggle with the *inner animal*. The latter is the instinctual " animal Soul", and is the hotbed of those passions which, as just shown, are lulled instead of being killed, and locked up in their breasts by some imprudent enthusiasts. Do they still hope to turn thereby the muddy stream of the animal sewer into the crystalline waters of life? And where, on what neutral ground, can they be imprisoned so as not to affect man? The fierce passions of love and lust are still alive, and they are allowed to still remain in the place of their birth—*that same animal soul*; for both the higher and

the lower portions of the "Human Soul"
or Mind reject such inmates, though they
cannot avoid being tainted with them as
neighbours. The "High Self" or Spirit
is as unable to assimilate such feeling as
water to get mixed with oil or unclean
liquid tallow. It is thus the mind alone—
the sole link and medium between the man
of earth and the Higher Self—that is the
only sufferer, and which is in incessant
danger of being dragged down by those
passions that may be reawakened at any
moment, and perish in the abyss of matter.
And how can it ever attune itself to the
divine harmony of the highest Principle,
when that harmony is destroyed by the
mere presence, within the Sanctuary in preparation, of such animal passions? How
can harmony prevail and conquer, when

the soul is stained and distracted with the turmoil of passions and the terrestrial desires of the bodily senses, or even of the " Astral man "?

For this " Astral "—the shadowy " double " (in the animal as in man)—is not the companion of the *divine Ego* but of the *earth body*. It is the link between the personal SELF, the lower consciousness of *Manas* and the Body, and is the vehicle of *transitory, not of immortal life*. Like the shadow projected by man, it follows his movements and impulses slavishly and mechanically, and leans therefore to matter without ever ascending to Spirit. It is only when the power of the passions is dead altogether, and when they have been crushed and annihilated in the retort of an unflinching will; when not only all the lusts and longings of the flesh are dead, but also the recognition of the personal Self is killed out and the "Astral" has been reduced in consequence to a cipher, that the Union with the "Higher Self" can take place. Then when the "Astral" reflects only the conquered man, the still living but no more the longing, selfish personality, then the brilliant *Augoeides*, the divine SELF, can vibrate in conscious harmony with both the poles of the human Entity—the man of matter purified, and the ever pure Spiritual Soul—and stand in the presence of the MASTER SELF, the Christos of the mystic Gnostic, blended, merged into, and one with IT for ever.[1]

[1] Those who would feel inclined to see three *Egos* in one man will show themselves unable to perceive the metaphysical meaning. Man is a trinity composed of Body, Soul and Spirit; but *man* is nevertheless *one*,

How, then, can it be thought possible for a man to enter the " strait gate " of occultism when his daily and hourly thoughts are bound up with worldly things, desires of possession and power, with lust, ambition, and duties which, however honourable, are still of the earth, earthly? Even the love for wife and family—the purest as the most unselfish of human affection—is a barrier to *real* occultism. For whether we take as an example the holy love of a mother for her child, or that of a husband for his wife, even in these feelings, when analysed to the very bottom, and thoroughly sifted, there is still *selshness* in the first, and an *egoisme a deux* in the second instance.

and is surely not his body. It is the latter which is the property, the transitory clothing of the man. The three ' EGOS " are MAN in his three aspects on the astral, intellectual or psychic, and the Spiritual planes, or states.

What mother would not sacrifice without
a moment's hesitation hundreds and thou-
sands of lives for that of the child of her
heart? and what lover or true husband
would not break the happiness of every other
man and woman around him to satisfy the
desire of one whom he loves? This is but
natural, we shall be told. Quite so, in the
light of the code of human affections; less
so, in that of divine universal love. For,
while the heart is full of thoughts for a little
group of *selves*, near and dear to us, how
shall the rest of mankind fare in our souls?
What percentage of love and care will there
remain to bestow on the " great orphan "?
And how shall the " still small voice " make
itself heard in a soul entirely occupied with
its own privileged tenants? What room is
there left for the needs of Humanity *en bloc*

to impress themselves upon, or even receive a speedy response? And yet, he who would profit by the wisdom of the universal mind, has to reach it through *the whole of Humanity* without distinction of race, complexion, religion, or social status. It is *altruism*, not *ego-ism* even in its most legal and noble conception, that can lead the unit to merge its little Self in the Universal Selves. It is to *these* needs and to this work that the true disciple of true Occultism has to devote himself if he would obtain *theo*-sophy, divine Wisdom and Knowledge.

The aspirant has to choose absolutely between the life of the world and the life of occultism. It is useless and vain to endeavour to unite the two, for no one can serve two masters and satisfy both. No one can serve his body and the higher Soul, and do his family duty and his universal duty, without depriving either one or the other of its rights; for he will either lend his ear to the " still small voice " and fail to hear the cries of his little ones, or, he will listen but to the wants of the latter and remain deaf to the voice of Humanity. It would be a ceaseless, a maddening struggle for almost any married man, who would pursue *true* practical Occultism, instead of its *theoretical* philosophy. For he would find himself ever hesitating between the voice of the impersonal divine love of Humanity, and that of the personal, terrestrial love. And this could only lead him to fail in one or the other, or perhaps in both his duties. Worse than this. For, *whoever indulges, after having pledged himself to* OCCULTISM, *in the gratification of a terrestrial love or lust,* must feel an almost immediate result—that of being irresistibly dragged from the impersonal divine state down to the lower plane of matter. Sensual, or even mental, self-gratification involves the immediate loss of the powers of spiritual discernment; the voice of the MASTER can no longer be distinguished from that of one's passions, *or even that of a Dugpa*; the right from wrong; sound morality from mere casuistry. The Dead Sea fruit assumes the most glorious mystic appearance, only to turn to ashes on the lips, and to gall in the heart, resulting in:

> " Depth ever deepening, darkness darkening still;
> Folly for wisdom, guilt for innocence;
> Anguish for rapture, and for hope despair."

And once being mistaken and having acted on their mistakes, most men shrink

from realising their error, and thus descend
deeper and deeper into the mire. And,
although it is the intention that decides
primarily whether *white* or *black* magic is
exercised, yet the results even of involuntary,
unconscious sorcery cannot fail to be pro-
ductive of bad Karma. Enough has been
said to show that *sorcery is any kind of evil
influence exercised upon other persons, who suffer,
or make other persons suffer, in consequence.*
Karma is a heavy stone splashed in the
quiet waters of Life; and it must produce
ever widening circles of ripples, carried
wider and wider, almost *ad infinitum*. Such
causes produced have to call forth effects
and these are evidenced in the just laws of
Retribution.

Much of this may be avoided if people
will only abstain from rushing into practices

neither the nature nor importance of which they understand. No one is expected to carry a burden beyond his strength and powers. There are " natural born magicians "; Mystics and Occultists by birth, and by right of direct inheritance from a series of incarnations and æons of suffering and failures. These are passion-proof, so to say. No fires of earthly origin can fan into a flame any of their senses or desires; no human voice can find response in their souls, except the great cry of Humanity. These only may be certain of success. But they can be met only far and wide, and they pass through the narrow gates of Occultism because they carry no personal luggage of human transitory sentiments along with them. They have got rid of the feeling of the lower personality, paralysed thereby the "astral" animal, and the golden, but narrow gate is thrown open before them. Not so with those who have to carry yet for several incarnations the burden of sins committed in previous lives, and even in their present existence. For such, unless they proceed with great caution, the golden gate of Wisdom may get transformed into the wide gate and the broad way "that leadeth unto destruction", and therefore "many be they that enter in thereby". This is the Gate of the Occult arts, practised for selfish motives and in the absence of the restraining and beneficent influence of ATMA-VIDYA. We are in the Kali Yuga and its fatal influence is a thousandfold more powerful in the West than it is in the East; hence the easy preys made by the Powers of the Age of Darkness in this cyclic struggle, and the many delusions under which the world is now labouring. One of these is the relative facility with which men fancy they can get at the "Gate" and cross the threshold of Occultism without any great sacrifice. It is the dream of most Theosophists, one inspired by desire for power and personal selfishness, and it is not such feelings that can ever lead them to the coveted goal. For, as well said by one believed to have sacrificed himself for Humanity—" narrow is the gate and straitened the way that leadeth unto life" eternal, and therefore "few be they that find it". So strait indeed, that at the bare mention of some of the preliminary difficulties the affrighted Western candidates turn back and retreat with a shudder. . . .

Let them stop here and attempt no more in their great weakness. For if while turning their backs on the narrow gate, they are dragged by their desire for the Occult one step in the direction of the broad and more inviting Gates of that golden mystery which glitters in the light of illusion, woe to them! It can lead only to Dugpaship, and they will be sure to find themselves very soon landed on that *Via Fatale* of the *Inferno*, over whose portal Dante read the words:

> *Per me si va nella citta dolente*
> *Per me si va nell' eterno dolore*
> *Per me si va tra la perduta gente. . .*

SOME PRACTICAL
SUGGESTIONS
FOR DAILY LIFE

PREFACE

PREFACE

THE quotations of which the following article is composed were not originally extracted with a view to publication, and may therefore appear somewhat disjointed.

They were first published as a *Theosophical Sifting*, in the hope that readers might take the hint, and make daily books of extracts for themselves, thus preserving a lasting record of the books read, and rendering their reading of practical value. By following this plan, the reader would concentrate in a brief space whatever has appealed to him as being the essence of the book.

The plan of reading a set of quotations each morning, trying to live up to them during the day, and meditating upon them in leisure moments, is also suggested as helpful to the earnest student.

¶ SOME PRACTICAL SUGGESTIONS

I

RISE early, as soon as you are awake, without lying idly in bed, half-waking and half-dreaming. Then earnestly pray that all mankind may be spiritually regenerated, that those who are struggling on the path of truth may be encouraged by your prayers and work more earnestly and successfully and that you may be strengthened and not yield to the seductions of the senses. Picture before your mind the form of your Master as engaged in Samadhi. Fix it before you, fill in all the details, think of him with reverence, and pray that all mistakes of omission and commission may be

5

forgiven. This will greatly facilitate concentration, purify your heart, and do much more. Or reflect upon the defects of your character: *thoroughly realise their evils and the transient pleasures they give you,* and firmly *will* that you shall try your best not to yield to them the next time. This self-analysis and bringing yourself before the bar of your own conscience facilitates, in a degree hitherto undreamt of, your spiritual progress. When you bathe, exercise, during the whole time your will, that your moral impurities should be washed away with those of your body. In your relations with others observe the following rules. 1. Never do anything which you are not bound to do as your duty; that is, any unnecessary thing. *Before* you do a thing, think whether it is your duty to do it. 2. *Never speak an unnecessary word.* Think of the effects your words might produce before you give utterance to them. *Never allow yourself to violate your principles by the force of your company.* 3. Never allow any unnecessary or vain thought to occupy your mind. This is more easily said than done. You cannot make your mind a blank all at once. So in the beginning try to prevent evil or idle thoughts by occupying your mind with the analysis of your own faults, or the contemplation of the Perfect Ones. 4. During meals exercise your will, that your food should be properly digested and build for you a body in harmony with your spiritual aspirations, and not create evil passion and wicked thoughts. Eat only when you are hungry and drink when you are thirsty, and *never otherwise.* If some particular preparation attracts your palate, do not allow yourself to be seduced into taking it simply to gratify that craving. Remember that the pleasure you derive from it had no existence some seconds before, and that it will cease to exist some seconds afterwards; that it is a transient pleasure, that that which is a pleasure now will turn into pain if you take it in large quantities; that it gives pleasure only to the tongue; that if you are put to a great trouble to get that thing, and if you allow yourself to be seduced by it, you will not be ashamed at any thing to get it; that while there is another object that can give you eternal bliss, this centering your affections on a transient thing is sheer folly; that *you* are neither the body nor the sense, and therefore the pleasure and the pains which *these* endure can never affect you really, and so on. Practise the same train of reasoning in the case of every other temptation, and, though you will often fail, yet you will achieve a surer success. *Do not read much.* If you read for ten minutes, reflect for as many hours. Habituate yourself to solitude, and to remaining alone with your thoughts.

Accustom yourself to the thought that *no one beside yourself can assist you*, and wean away your affections from all things gradually. Before you sleep, pray as you did in the morning. *Review the actions of the day*, and see wherein you have failed, and resolve that you will not fail in them tomorrow.[1]

---

[1] *Theosophist*, August '89, p. 647.

II

THE right motive for seeking self-knowledge is that which pertains to *knowledge* and not to *self*. Self-knowledge is worth seeking by virtue of its being knowledge, and not by virtue of its pertaining to self. The main requisite for acquiring self-knowledge is *pure love*. Seek knowledge for pure love, and self-knowledge eventually crowns the effort. The fact of a student growing impatient is proof positive that he works for reward, and not for love, and that in its turn proves that he does not deserve the great victory in store for those who really work for pure love.[1]

The "God" in us—that is to say, the Spirit of Love and Truth, Justice and

[1] *Theosophist*, August '89, p. 663.

Wisdom, Goodness and Power—should be our only true and permanent *Love*, our only reliance in everything, our only *Faith*, which, standing firm as a rock, can for ever be trusted; our only *Hope*, which will never fail us if all other things perish; and the only object which we must seek to obtain, by our Patience, waiting contentedly until our evil Karma has been exhausted and the divine Redeemer will reveal to us his presence within our soul. The door through which he enters is called *Contentment*; for he who is discontented with himself is discontented with the law that made him such as he is; and as God is *Himself* the Law, God will not come to those that are discontented with Him.[1] If we admit that we

---

[1] *Theosophical Siftings*, No. 8, vol. ii, p. 9, Hartmann.

are in the stream of evolution, then *each* circumstance *must* be to us quite right. And in our failure to perform set acts should be our greatest help, for we can in no other way learn that calmness which Krishna insists upon. If all our plans succeeded, then no contrasts would appear to us. Also those plans we make may all be made ignorantly, and thus wrongly, and kind Nature will not permit us to carry them out. We get no blame for the plan, but we may acquire karmic demerit by not accepting the impossibility of achieving. If you are at all cast down, then by just that much are your thoughts lessened in power. *One could be confined in a prison and yet be a worker for the cause.* So I pray you to remove from your mind any distaste for present circumstances. If you can succeed in looking at it all *as just what you in fact desired*,[1] then it will act not only as a strengthener of your thoughts, but will act reflexly on your body and make it stronger.[2]

To act and act wisely when the time for action comes, to wait and wait patiently when it is time for repose, put man in accord with the rising and falling tides (of affairs), so that with nature and law at his back, and truth and beneficence as his beacon light, he may accomplish wonders. Ignorance of this law results in periods of unreasoning enthusiasm on the one hand, and depression and even despair on the other. Man thus becomes the victim of the tides when he should be their Master.[3]

[1] "*You*" meaning the Higher Self. We *are* as we make ourselves.

[2] *Path*, August '89, p. 131.

[3] *Path*, July '89, p. 107.

Have patience, Candidate, as one who fears no failure, courts no success.[1]

Accumulated energy cannot be annihilated, it must be transferred to other forms, or be transformed into other modes of motion; it cannot remain for ever inactive and yet continue to exist. It is useless to attempt to *resist* a passion which we cannot control. If its accumulating energy is not led into other channels, it will grow until it becomes stronger than will, and stronger than reason. *To control it*, you must lead it into another and *higher* channel. Thus a love for something vulgar may be changed by turning it into a love for something high, and *vice may be changed into virtue by changing its aim.* Passion is blind, it goes where it is led, and reason is a safer guide for it than the

[1] *Voice of the Silence.*

instinct. Stored up anger (or love) *will* find some object upon which to spend its fury, else it may produce an explosion destructive to its possessor; *tranquillity follows a storm*. The ancients said that nature suffers no vacuum. We cannot destroy or annihilate a passion. If it is driven away, another elemental influence will take its place. We should therefore not attempt to destroy the low without putting something in its place, but we should displace the low by the high; vice by virtue, and superstition by knowledge.[1]

III

LEARN that there is no cure for desire, no cure for the love of reward, no cure for the

[1] *Magic*, p. 126, Hartmann.

misery of longing, save in the fixing of the sight and hearing on that which is invisible and soundless.[1]

A man must believe in his innate power of progress. A man must refuse to be terrified by his greater nature, and must not be drawn back by his lesser or material self.[2]

All the past shows us that difficulty is no excuse for dejection, much less for despair, else the world would have been without the many wonders of civilisation.[3]

Strength to step forward is the primary need of him who has chosen his path. Where is this to be found? Looking round, it is not hard to see where other men find

[1] *Light on the Path*, Karma.

[2] Comments, *Light on the Path*.

[3] *Through the Gates of Gold*, p. 69.

their strength. Its source is profound
conviction.[1]

Abstain because it is right to abstain, not
that yourself shall be kept clean.[2]

The man who wars against himself and
wins the battle can do it only when he
knows that in that war he is doing the one
thing which is worth doing.[3]

"Resist not evil," that is, do not complain of or feel anger against the inevitable
disagreeables of life. *Forget yourself* (in working for others). If men revile, persecute,
or wrong one, why resist? In the resistance
we create greater evils.[4]

The immediate work, whatever it may
be, has the abstract claim of duty, and its

---

[1] *Op. cit.*, p. 87.
[2] *Light on the Path.*
[3] *Through the Gates of Gold*, p. 118.
[4] *Path*, August '87, p. 151.

relative importance or non-importance is not to be considered at all.[1]

The best remedy for evil is not the suppression, but the elimination of desire, and this can best be accomplished by keeping the mind constantly steeped in things divine. The knowledge of the Higher Self is snatched away by engaging the mind in brooding over or contemplating with pleasure the objects which correspond to the unruly sense.[2]

Our own nature is so base, proud, ambitious, and so full of its own appetites, judgments, and opinions, that if temptations restrained it not, it would be undone without remedy; therefore are we tempted to the

---

[1] *Lucifer,* Feb. '88, p. 478.

[2] **Page 60,** *Bhagavad Gita.* (All quotations are taken from Mohini's translation.)

end that we may know ourselves and be
humble. Know that the greatest temptation is to be without temptation, where-
fore be glad when it assaults thee, and
with resignation, peace, and constancy
resist it.[1]

Feel that you have nothing to do *for
yourself*, but that certain charges are laid
upon you by the Deity, which you must
fulfil. Desire God and *not anything that
he can give*.[2] Whatever there is to do, *has*
to be done, but not for the sake of enjoying
the fruit of action.[3] If all one's acts are
performed with the full conviction that they
are of no value to the actor, but are to be
done simply because they *have* to be done—

[1] Molinos, *Spiritual Guide*.
[2] P. 182, *Bhagavad Gita*.
[3] Introduction, *Bhagavad Gita*.

in other words, because it is in our nature to act—then the personality of egotism in us will grow weaker and weaker until it comes to rest, permitting the knowledge revealing the True Self to shine out in all its splendour.

One must not allow joy or pain to shake one from one's fixed purpose.[1]

Until the master chooses you to come to him, *be* with humanity, and unselfishly work for its progress and advancement. This alone can bring true satisfaction.[2]

Knowledge increases in proportion to its *use*—that is, the more we teach the more we learn. Therefore, Seeker after Truth, with the *faith* of a little child and the will of an Initiate, give of your store to him who

[1] Comments, *Light on the Path.*

[2] *Path*, December '86, p. 279.

hath not wherewithal to comfort him on his journey.[1]

A disciple must fully recognise that the very thought of individual rights is only the outcome of the venomous quality of the snake of Self. He must never regard another man as a person who can be criticised or condemned, nor may he raise his voice in self-defence or excuse.[2]

No man is your enemy, no man is friend. *All alike are your teachers*.[3] One must no longer work for the gain of any *benefit*, temporal or spiritual, but to fulfil the law of being which is the righteous will of God.[4]

---

[1] *Path*, Dec. '86, p. 280

[2] *Lucifer*, Jan. '83, p. 832

[3] *Light on the Path*.

[4] *Bhagavad Gita*. Introduction.

IV

LIVE neither in the present nor the future, but in the *eternal*. The giant weed (of evil) cannot flower there; this blot upon existence is wiped out by the very atmosphere of eternal thought.[1] Purity of heart is a necessary condition for the attainment of " Knowledge of the Spirit." There are two principal means by which this purification may be attained. First, drive away persistently every bad thought; secondly, preserve an even mind under all conditions, *never be agitated or irritated at anything*. It will be found that these two means of purification are best promoted by *devotion* and *charity*. We must *not* sit idle and make no attempt to advance because we do

[1] *Light on the Path*, Rule 4.

not feel ourselves pure. *Let everyone aspire,* and let them work in right earnest, but they must work in the right way, and the first step of that way is to purify the heart.[1]

The mind requires purification whenever anger is felt or a falsehood is told, or the *faults of another needlessly disclosed*; whenever anything is said or done for the purpose of flattery, or anyone is deceived by the insincerity of a speech or an act.[2]

Those who wish for salvation ought to avoid lust, anger and greed, and cultivate courageous obedience to the Scriptures, study of Spiritual philosophy, and *perseverance* in its practical realisation.[3]

[1] *Theosophist*, Oct. '88, p. 44.
[2] *Bhagavad Gita*, p. 325.
[3] *Ibid.*, p. 240.

He who is led by selfish considerations cannot enter a heaven where personal considerations do not exist. *He who does not care for Heaven, but is contented where he is, is already in Heaven,* while the discontented will in vain clamour for it. To be without personal desires is to be free and happy, and " Heaven " can mean nothing else but a state in which freedom and happiness exist. The man who performs beneficial acts induced by a hope of reward is not happy unless the reward is obtained, and if his reward is obtained his happiness ends. There can be no permanent rest and happiness as long as there is some work to be done, and not accomplished, and the fulfilment of duties brings its own reward.[1]

[1] *Magic,* Intro., p. 34, Hartmann.

He who thinks himself holier than another, he who has any pride in his own exemption from vice or folly, he who believes himself wise, or in any way superior to his fellowmen, is incapable of discipleship. A man must become as a little child before he can enter the Kingdom of Heaven. Virtue and wisdom are sublime things, but if they create pride and a consciousness of separateness from the rest of humanity, they are only the snakes of self reappearing in a finer form. The sacrifice or surrender of the *heart* of man *and its emotions* is the first of the rules; it involves " the attaining of an equilibrium which cannot be shaken by personal emotion." Put, without delay, your good intentions into practice, never leaving a single one to remain only an intention. Our only true course is to let the motive for action be in the action itself, never in its reward; not to be incited to action by the hope of the result, nor yet indulge a propensity to inertness.

Through *faith* [1] the *heart* is purified from passion and folly; from that comes mastery over the *body*, and, *last of all*, subjugation of the senses. [2]

The characteristics of the illuminated sage are, *1st*, he is free from all desires, [3] and *knows* that the true Ego or Supreme Spirit alone is bliss, all else is pain. *2nd*, that he is free from attachment and repulsion towards whatever may befall him, and that he acts without determination. *Lastly* comes

[1] *i.e., knowledge,* and this comes by the practice of unselfishness and kindness.

[2] P. 95, *Bhagavad Gita.*

[3] This can best be accomplished by keeping the mind constantly steeped in things divine.

the subjugation of the *senses*, which is useless, and frequently injurious as breeding
hypocrisy and spiritual pride, without the
second, and that again is not of much use
without the first.[1]

He who does not practise altruism, he
who is not prepared to share his last morsel [2]
with a weaker or poorer than himself, he
who neglects to help his brother man, of
whatever race, nation, or creed, *wherever
and whenever* he meets suffering, and who
turns a deaf ear to the cry of human
misery; he who hears an innocent person
slandered, and does not undertake his
defence as he would undertake his own,
is no Theosophist.

[1] P. 61, *Bhagavad Gita.*

[2] This must be taken in its *widest* sense also, *i.e.*
spiritual knowledge, etc.

V

No man does right who gives up the unmistakable duties of life, resting on Divine command. He who performs duties, thinking that if they are *not* performed some evil will come to him, or that their performance will remove difficulties from his path, works for result. Duties should simply be done because commanded by God, who may at any time command their abandonment. So long as the restlessness of our nature is not reduced to tranquillity we must work, consecrating to the Deity all fruit of our action, and attribute to Him the power to perform works rightly. The *true* life of man is *rest in identity with the Supreme Spirit.*

This life is not brought into existence by any act of ours, it is a reality, " the truth ",

and is *altogether independent of us.* The
realisation of the non-existence of all that
seems opposed to this truth is *a new consciousness* and not an act. Man's liberation
is in no way related to his acts. In so far
as acts promote the realisation of our utter
inability to emancipate ourselves from con-
ditioned existence, they are of use; after
this stage is realised acts become obstacles
rather than helps. Those who work in
obedience to Divine commands, knowing
that the power thus to work is a gift of
God, and no part of man's self-conscious
nature, attain to freedom from the need of
action. Then the pure heart is filled by the
truth, and identity with the Deity is per-
ceived. A man must first get rid of the
idea that *he himself* really does anything,
knowing that all actions take place in the

" three natural qualities," [1] and *not* in the soul at all. Then he must place all his actions on *devotion*. That is, sacrifice all his actions to the Supreme and not to himself. He must either set *himself* up as the God to whom he sacrifices, or the *other* real God—Ishvara; and all his acts and aspirations are done either for himself or for the All. *Here comes in the importance of motive.* For if he performs great deeds of valour, or of benefit to man, or acquires knowledge so as to assist man, and is moved to that merely because he thus thinks *he* will attain salvation, he is only acting for his own benefit, and is therefore sacrificing *to himself*. Therefore he must be devoted inwardly to the All; knowing that *he* is *not* the doer of the actions, but the *mere witness*

---

[1] *i.e.* the three *gunas*.

of them. As he is in a mortal body he is
affected by doubts which *will* spring up.
When they do arise, it is because he is ignorant about something. He should therefore be able to disperse doubt "by the
sword of knowledge." For if he has a ready
answer to some doubt he disperses that
much. *All doubts come from the lower nature,*
and *never* in any case from the higher nature.
Therefore as he becomes more and more
devoted he is able to know more and more
clearly the knowledge residing in his Sattva
(goodness) nature. For it says: " A man
who is perfected in *devotion* (or who persists
in its cultivation) finds spiritual knowledge
spontaneously in himself in progress of
time." Also, " A man of doubtful mind
enjoys neither this world nor the other (the
Deva world), nor final beatitude." The

last sentence is to destroy the idea that if there is in us this Higher Self it will, even if we are indolent and doubtful, triumph over the necessity for knowledge and lead us to final beatitude in common with the whole stream of mankind.[1]

True prayer is the contemplation of all sacred things, of their application to ourselves, our daily life and actions, accompanied by the most heartfelt and intense desire to make their influence stronger and our lives better and nobler, that some knowledge of them may be vouchsafed to us. All such thoughts must be closely interwoven with a consciousness of the Supreme and Divine Essence from which all things have sprung.[2]

[1] *Path*, July '89, p. 109.
[2] *Path*, Aug. '89, p. 159.

Spiritual culture is attained through *concentration*. It must be continued daily and *every moment to be of use*. *Meditation* has been defined as " the cessation of active external thought." *Concentration* is the entire life-tendency to a given end. For example, a devoted mother is one who consults the interests of her children and *all* branches of their interests in and before all things; not one who sits down to think fixedly about *one* branch of their interests all the day. Thought has a self-reproductive power, and when the mind is held steadily to one idea it becomes coloured by it, and, as we may say, all the correlates of that thought arise within the mind. Hence the mystic obtains knowledge about any object of which he thinks constantly in fixed contemplation. Here is the rationale of Krishna's words:

"Think constantly of me; depend on me alone, and *thou shalt surely come to me*." Life is the great teacher: it is the great manifestation of Soul, and Soul manifests the Supreme. Hence all methods are good and all are but parts of the great aim, which is Devotion. "Devotion is success in action", says the *Bhagavad Gita*. The psychic powers, as they come, must also be used, for they reveal laws. But their value must not be exaggerated, nor must their danger be ignored. He who relies on them is like a man who gives way to pride and triumph because he has reached the first wayside station on the peaks he has set out to climb.[1]

[1] *Path*, July, 89, p. 111.

VI

IT is an eternal law that man cannot be redeemed by a power *external to himself*. Had this been possible, an angel might long ago have visited the earth, uttered heavenly truths, and, by manifesting the faculties of a spiritual nature, proved a hundred facts to the consciousness of man of which he is ignorant.[1]

Crime is committed in the Spirit as truly as in the deeds of the body. He who for *any* cause hates another, who loves revenge, and will not forgive an injury, is full of the spirit of murder, though none may know it. He who bows before false creeds, and crushes his conscience at the bidding of any institution, blasphemes his own divine soul,

[1] *Spirit of the Testament*, p. 508.

and therefore " takes the name of God in vain " though he never utters an oath. He who desires and is in sympathy with the mere pleasures of sense, either in or out of the married relation, is the real adulterer. He who deprives any of his fellows of the light, the good, the help, the assistance he can wisely give them, and lives for the accumulation of material things, for his own personal gratification, is the real robber; and he who steals from his fellows the precious possession of character by slander, and any sort of misrepresentation, is no less a thief, and one of the most guilty kind.[1]

If men were only honest with themselves and *kindly disposed* towards others, a tremendous change would take place in

[1] *Spirit of the Testament*, p. 513.

their estimate of the value of life, and of the things of this life.[1]

DEVELOP THOUGHT. Strive, by concentrating the whole force of your soul, to shut the door of your mind to all stray thoughts, allowing none to enter but those calculated to reveal to you the unreality of sense-life, and the Peace of the Inner World. Ponder day and night over the unreality of all your surroundings and of yourself. The springing up of *evil* thoughts is less injurious than that of idle and indifferent ones. Because as to evil thoughts you are always on your guard, and, having determined to fight and conquer them, this determination helps to develop the will power. Indifferent thoughts, however, serve merely to distract the attention and waste energy. The first great basic

[1] *Theosophist*, July '89, p. 590.

7

delusion you have to get over is the identification of yourself with the physical body. Begin to think of this body as nothing better than the house you have to live in for a time, and then you will never yield to its temptations. Try also with consistent attempts to conquer the prominent weaknesses of your nature by developing thought in the direction that will kill each particular passion. After your first efforts you will begin to feel an indescribable vacuum and blankness in your heart; fear not, but regard this as the soft twilight heralding the rise of the sun of spiritual bliss. Sadness is not an evil. Complain not; what seem to be sufferings and obstacles are often in reality the mysterious efforts of nature to help you in your work if you can manage them properly. Look upon *all* circumstances with the gratitude of a pupil.[1] All complaint is a rebellion against the law of progress. That which is to be shunned is *pain not yet come*. The past cannot be changed or amended; that which belongs to the experiences of the present cannot and *should* not be shunned; but alike to be shunned are *disturbing anticipations* or *fears of the future* and every act or impulse that may cause present or future pain to ourselves or others.[2]

VII

THERE is no more valuable thing possessed by any individual than an exalted ideal towards which he continually aspires, and after which he moulds his thoughts and

[1] *Theosophical Siftings*, No. 3, vol. 2, '89.
[2] Patanjali's *Yoga Aphorisms*.

feelings, and forms, as best he may, his life. If he thus strives to *become* rather than to *seem*, he cannot fail to continually approach nearer his aim. He will not, however, reach this point without a struggle, nor will the real progress that he is conscious of making fill him with conceit or self-righteousness; for if his ideal be high, and his progress towards it real, he will be the rather humiliated than puffed up. The possibilities of further advancement, and the conception of still higher planes of being that open before him, will not dampen his ardour, though they will surely kill his conceit. It is just this conception of the vast possibilities of human life that is needed to kill out *ennui*, and to convert apathy into zest. Life thus becomes worth living for its own sake when its mission becomes plain, and its splendid opportunities are once appreciated. The most direct and certain way of reaching this higher plane is the cultivation of the *principle of altruism*, both in *thought and life*. Narrow indeed is the sweep of vision that is limited to self, and that measures all things by the principle of self-interest, for while the soul is thus self-limited it is impossible for it to conceive of any high ideal, or to approach any higher plane of life. The conditions of such advancement lie *within* rather than without, and are fortunately made independent of circumstances and conditions in life. The opportunity therefore is offered to *everyone* of advancing from height to height of being, and of thus working with nature in the accomplishment of the evident purpose of life.[1]

[1] *Man*, J. Buck, p. 106.

If we believe that the object of life is simply to render our material self satisfied, and to keep it in comfort, and that material comfort confers the highest state of possible happiness, we mistake the low for the high, and an illusion for the truth. Our material mode of life is a consequence of the material constitution of our bodies. We are " worms of the earth " because we cling with all our aspirations to earth. If we can enter upon a path of evolution, by which we become less material and more ethereal, a very different order of civilisation would be established. Things which now appear indispensable and necessary would cease to be useful; if we could transfer our consciousness with the velocity of thought from one part of the globe to another, the present modes of communication would be no longer required.

The deeper we sink into matter, the more material means for comfort will be needed; the *essential* and powerful god in man is *not material*, and independent of the restrictions laid upon matter. What are the *real* necessities of life? The answer to this question depends entirely on what we imagine to be necessary. Railways, steamers, etc. are now a necessity to us, and yet millions of people have lived long and happily, knowing nothing about them. To one man a dozen palaces may appear to be an indispensable necessity, to another a carriage, another a pipe, and so on. But *all such necessities are only such as man himself has created*. They make the state in which man now is agreeable to him, and *tempt him to remain* in the state, and to desire nothing higher. They may even hinder his development instead of advancing it. Everything material must cease to become a necessity if we would really advance spiritually. It is the *craving* and the *wasting of thought* for the augmentation of the pleasures of the lower life which prevent men entering the higher one.[1]

[1] *Magic*, Hartmann, p. 61.